The Mystery of Sleep

by Alvin and Virginia Silverstein

Illustrated by Nelle Davis

Little, Brown and Company

Boston   Toronto

First Edition

Library of Congress Cataloging-in-Publication Data
Silverstein, Alvin.
    The mystery of sleep.

    Summary: Discusses the subject of sleep, including animal
sleep, dreams, nightmares, and sleep problems.
    1. Sleep — Physiological aspects — Juvenile literature.
[1. Sleep 2. Dreams] I. Silverstein, Virginia B.
II. Davis, Nelle, ill. III. Title.
QP425.S586   1987   612'.821   86-20104
ISBN 0-316-79117-2

BP

Published simultaneously in Canada
by Little, Brown & Company (Canada) Limited

Printed in the United States of America

Contents

The Mystery
of Sleep

★————————————————★

What happens to you while you are asleep?

You lie down in bed at night and close your eyes. Then — just a short time later it seems — you open your eyes, and it's morning. Eight hours may have gone by — a whole third of a day! What were you doing all that time? Were you just turned off like a light switch? Sleep can seem very mysterious.

1

When you wake up, you may not remember anything about what happened during the night. Or perhaps you wake up and remember a dream.

Some dreams are pleasant. Maybe you are eating an ice cream cone in your dream, or riding on a circus pony. It seems so real! When you first wake up, you can almost taste the creamy-cold sweetness of the ice cream melting in your mouth. You can smell the roasting peanuts at the circus, and see the bright colors of the clowns' costumes. You feel so good, you wish you could go back into the dream world and enjoy it some more.

But sometimes you have bad dreams. Maybe a tiger is chasing you. It is getting closer — about to pounce on you! You are very frightened when you awaken. You think the tiger is real — it's right there in bed with you! You turn on the light and look around for a place to hide. A moment later you realize there isn't any tiger in your bedroom. It was never really there at all; the tiger was in your mind.

Only part of the night is spent dreaming. What happens the rest of the night?

As you are falling asleep, you lie very quietly. But you do not stay still while you are sleeping. You turn over many times. Sometimes you sleep on your stomach, sometimes on your back, sometimes on your side. You may talk in your sleep. You may laugh or cry.

Some people get out of bed and walk around while they are asleep. They are sleepwalking. They do not know they are out of bed. They can walk around and do things even though they are sound asleep. If they wake up, they will be very surprised to see where they are.

When you are sleeping, you still know a little about what is going on in your room. If someone talks to you, you may answer (but you won't remember it after you wake up). If it gets cold, you may pull up the covers. You can feel the edge of the bed and keep

yourself from falling off. But all the while, you are sound asleep.

Why do we spend a third of our lives lying in bed, tuning out nearly everything around us? How do people fall asleep, and how do they wake up? And what is going on in the body in between? Is sleep necessary, or could you learn to do without it? Just what is this mysterious thing called sleep?

Animals Sleep, Too

★——————————————————————————★

You sleep every night. So do your mother and father. So does everybody you know.

Animals sleep, too.

Birds sleep perched on tree branches. Their feet lock tightly onto the branch so that they will not fall, even when they are sound asleep. Most birds sleep during the night. But owls sleep during the day and hunt at night.

Some animals, such as horses, sleep standing up.

But most animals curl up in some cozy place to sleep.

Have you ever heard people talk about taking *catnaps*? What they mean is that they doze off for a short, refreshing sleep, to take a break from their daytime duties. If you've ever had a cat, you can guess why these daytime sleeps are called *cat*naps. Cats can fall asleep almost anywhere, and they spend a lot of time sleeping — as much as fourteen hours a day. Like people, cats move around when they are sleeping. Sometimes a cat sleeps curled up in a little ball, with its tail wrapped neatly around it. Sometimes it is stretched out limply like a fur rug. And sometimes it lies on its back with its paws in the air.

Did you ever watch a dog sleeping? It wiggles its nose and makes funny faces. It makes little noises, and it may even bark. The dog seems to be dreaming.

In general, animals that hunt are sound sleepers, especially when they have a safe place to sleep. They sleep deeply, and they sleep for a long time. Wolves sleep in their dens. So do bears. In fact, bears sleep through the whole winter. They spend summer and fall eating and getting fat, and then they curl up in their dens and sleep until spring. They go for months without eating, living on the fat stored in their bodies.

Animals that are hunted are usually rather light sleepers. Sheep, goats, and donkeys can go for a long time without sleeping at all. When they do sleep, they take short naps and wake up easily. Rabbits sleep for a few minutes at a time. Between their short naps they are busy eating and watching out for their enemies.

A few hunted animals, however, can sleep soundly. But these are all animals that can hide in safe underground burrows while they are sleeping. Ground squirrels, for instance, sleep fourteen hours a day. And chipmunks sleep all winter. A chipmunk goes to bed for its winter sleep in a snug burrow. Before it goes

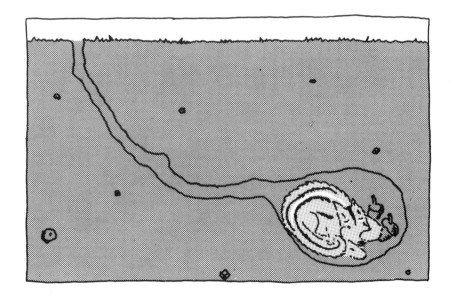

to sleep, it gathers a supply of nuts. During the winter months it wakes up from time to time, takes a snack from its food supplies, and goes back to sleep.

Scientists have learned a lot about what happens during sleep by studying animals. They also study human sleep. When you go to bed tonight, scientists in a number of laboratories will be staying awake to watch people sleeping.

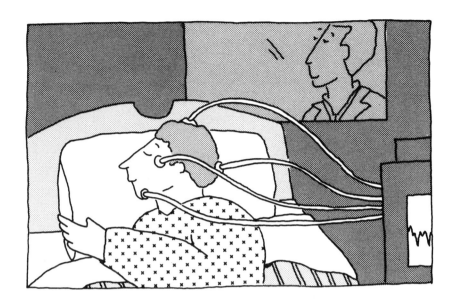

Studying Sleep

How could scientists find out what happens while you are sleeping, when you don't even know what is going on yourself? For a long time the scientists could only guess. But then an important discovery was made. It was found that there is electricity in the brain.

Does that sound scary? When your brain is working, electric currents are flowing along your brain cells. It is only a tiny bit of electricity, though. You can't feel it. You won't get a shock if you touch your forehead.

Scientists can measure this electricity from your brain. They don't have to open up your head to do it. They can pick up the electricity from the outside of the head. They paste little flat metal disks to the forehead and scalp. These disks, called *electrodes*, are about as big as a dime, and they are attached to wires. The wires are connected to a machine called an *electroencephalograph*, or *EEG* machine. This machine measures electricity from people's brains.

You can't get a shock from an EEG machine. All the electricity flows from the brain to the machine. No electricity flows from the machine to the brain.

The EEG machine writes down measurements on a long sheet of paper. EEG writing looks like long wiggly lines. The recordings from one night's sleep use up about half a mile of EEG paper!

Can you imagine going to sleep in a laboratory, with wires attached to your head and people watching you? Most people have trouble sleeping on the first night in a sleep lab. But by the second night, they can sleep very well — just as though they were home in their own beds. In fact, some people sleep better in the lab than they do in their own beds.

When you first lie down to sleep, the EEG machine traces out a special pattern of wiggly lines. It looks like a series of waves, one after another. Scientists call these waves *alpha waves*. They are traced out when a person is awake but quiet.

After a little while, the pattern of waves starts to change. The sleep researchers, watching the paper tape coming out of the EEG machine, know that you are falling asleep. It is a very light kind of sleep, easy to wake up from. If you wake up from a light sleep, you may not even think you were sleeping. You may say you were only thinking.

Gradually the pens tracing the wiggly lines on the paper slow down. Now they make a pattern of very slow waves called *delta waves*. When the EEG machine records delta waves from your brain, you are in

a very deep sleep, one that it is hard to wake up from. Even a loud noise probably would not wake you. Deep sleep is very restful. Your body is completely relaxed.

About an hour and a half into your sleep, the EEG writing changes again. The pens speed up, and the slow delta waves disappear. The wiggly lines look a lot like the ones that are recorded when you are awake and active. But you are not awake. You are sound asleep. Your body is limp — so limp that if you woke up, you would not be able to move for a minute or two. Your eyelids are still closed, but under them your eyes are moving back and forth. It looks as though you are watching a movie. If somebody woke you up right now, you would say you were dreaming. You would remember the dream very clearly, and you could tell all about what happened in it. But if you did not wake up until the dream was over, you probably would not remember it.

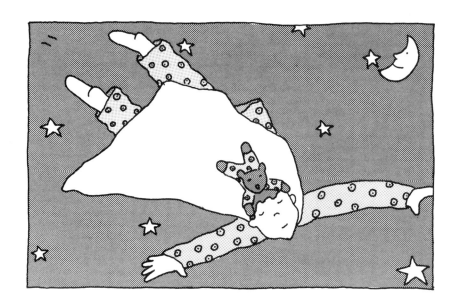

Dreams

★──────────────────────────────────────★

Scientists have a special name for dreaming sleep. They call it *REM* sleep. This name is an abbreviation. It comes from the first letters of the words *rapid eye movements* — which is what your eyes do while you are dreaming.

Your first dream of the night lasts for only a few minutes. Then you go back into a deep sleep. But all through the night, every hour and a half, you have another dream. Each dream is longer. You may have five or six dreams in a night. But probably you will not remember most of your dreams. You remember only the last dream you had — the one you were having when you woke up.

Dreams are very strange. They seem real, but things happen in them that could not happen in real life. You may be able to fly in a dream. Or you may be at home one minute and halfway around the world the next. You don't know how you got there, and you don't even care. The people and places in your dreams may be familiar ones, from your everyday life. Or they may be people and places from long ago, or from the future, or from a magic kingdom. A beautiful fairy godmother may suddenly turn into a monster. Sometimes you dream that you are somebody else. Or your dream may be all about other people, and you are watching their story as if it were a show on television.

Where do the things you dream about come from? You dream about things that happened during the day. You dream about pictures you have seen. You dream about stories you have heard. You dream about things you have read. Your mind puts these all together and makes stories out of them.

Sometimes things that happen to you while you are sleeping become part of your dreams. If you wet the bed, you may dream that you are swimming. You may dream that the telephone is ringing and then wake up to find that it is your alarm clock.

Some people use dreams to help them solve problems. Have you ever been worrying about something just before you went to bed and then found that you had an answer when you woke up in the morning? You will dream more than usual when you are worried. It seems that your brain works on your problems even while you are sleeping. Sometimes it can come up with good ideas. Some great scientific discoveries have been based on ideas that scientists got in dreams. And some wonderful poems and stories were made up in dreams and then written down when the authors woke up. (One famous poem that came from a dream is unfinished. A visitor came while the poet was writing it down, and after that he couldn't remember the rest.) When you are studying for a test, it is a good idea to study before bedtime. Then your mind will do some more studying while you are asleep. It will go over the facts you learned and perhaps even discover some new patterns and ideas.

Do the strange events in dreams mean anything? Some people think so. They think they are symbols that stand for things you are afraid to think about when you are awake. They believe that if you can remember your dreams and figure out what they mean, you will understand yourself better.

Other people think that dreams can predict the future. Some people have claimed that they have dreamed about a great fire or a big plane crash, and then it really happened. And a few people think their dreams will tell them the winning number for a lottery.

Scientists are not sure if any of these things are true, but they have their own ideas about dreams. They think that dreams give the brain a chance to sort through the events of the day. The brain compares them with older experiences and decides which ones are important enough to store away as memories. It also makes plans for the future. One scientist compares the brain to a computer. He says that during the day, when you have most of your experiences, the brain receives so much new information that it can't handle all of it at once. So, like a computer, it stores away most of the new information in a temporary memory. Then at night, when your eyes are closed, and there is not much going on around you, the brain has time to pull bits of new information out of the temporary memory and think about them. Dreams are the result of the brain's attempts to make sense out of the new data and relate them to what you already know.

No matter which theories about dreams are correct, we do know that something important goes on during dreaming. When sleepers in a sleep lab are awakened each time they start to dream, they feel bad the next day. They are grouchy and have trouble concentrating. And the next night, if they are allowed to dream all they want to, they spend much more time dreaming than usual. Some drugs used as *sleeping pills* cut down on dreaming time, and they have the same effects. A person who stops taking the sleeping pills may have many vivid dreams, including terrible nightmares, for a few nights afterward. The body seems to be trying to make up for the lost dreaming time.

Nightmares

★——★

Did you know that there are two different kinds of
bad dreams? Sleep experts call one kind *night terrors*.
You wake up suddenly, feeling very frightened. Your
heart is racing, and you are sweating and crying. You
may not be quite sure why you felt so scared. Or you
might say something like "I felt like I couldn't breathe —
something was smothering me." Or you may not remember anything at all. EEG recordings show that
night terrors occur during deep, slow-wave sleep. They

occur most often when you are very young, but usually they stop as you get older.

Nightmares are very vivid bad dreams. They occur during REM sleep, and if you wake up in the middle of one, you can remember it very clearly. If you are with someone who is sleeping but is moaning and crying and seems to be having a nightmare, you might be tempted to wake him or her up to "save" the person from the bad dream. Don't do it. A person who sleeps right through a nightmare will not remember it. But if you wake a person up during a nightmare, the bad feelings from the dream may stay with him or her for much of the day. And then the bad dream may come back again. Some people have the same dream over and over again. Sometimes this happens after a very bad experience. People who have been in a plane crash or who have fought in a war may relive the experience in their dreams for months or even years afterward. In another common kind of recurring nightmare, you have an important exam to take but haven't had a chance to study for it!

If you are having problems with nightmares, you can learn to control your dreams. Think about the dreams before you go to bed and tell yourself that this time you are going to be prepared. If a tiger is chasing you, then decide this time you won't try to run and hide. You'll turn and face the tiger, and you'll have a big spear you can throw at it. If that's not good enough, you can call your friends in the dream, and they will come and help you chase the tiger away. It takes a little practice, but gradually you can learn to take the fear out of your nightmares, and then they won't bother you anymore.

Who Needs Sleep?

Do you ever wish you did not have to go to bed at all?
There are so many interesting things to do when you
are awake, that you wish you could stay up all night.
Sometimes people do just that. They stay up all night,
studying for an exam, or finishing a project at work,
or just having fun at a late-night party.

It is not too hard to stay up past your bedtime if
you are doing something interesting. But after a time,
you suddenly feel very tired. Then if you stay up longer,

21

the tiredness passes, and you feel fine again. Later into the night, waves of tiredness may hit you again and again. Finally, when your normal waking-up time comes, you feel ready to start the new day — almost as if you had slept all night.

"Who needs sleep?" you think. But as the day goes by, waves of tiredness hit you again and again. Sometimes you may actually fall asleep for a minute or two, while you are sitting or standing up. Even when you are wide awake, you are not quite your normal self. You may find it hard to think and concentrate. You may make mistakes, and your reactions are slow. If somebody throws you a ball, you might let it hit you instead of catching it. And you are irritable. But the next day, after a good night's sleep, you are fine again.

People have tried staying up for more than one night. Some have even stayed up for a whole week. But they have found that people really do need sleep. After a few days without sleep, people have trouble thinking and remembering things. They get sick easily. They may start seeing things that aren't there, like monsters, or flames coming out of the walls. They may imagine that other people are plotting against them or trying to hurt them. People who have gone without sleep for a long time begin to act as if they were crazy. But a long, restful night's sleep is enough to bring them back to normal.

How much sleep does a person need? That depends on how old you are. Newborn babies need a lot of sleep — as much as eighteen to twenty-one hours out of every twenty-four. There are several reasons for this. One is that the body grows and repairs itself while a person is sleeping. Babies grow so fast that they need plenty of sleep. They spend a lot of time in REM sleep. If scientists are correct in believing that the brain sorts out experiences and stores away the important ones as memories when you dream, it would make sense that babies need to sleep a lot. Think how many new experiences a baby has: people's faces, voices, colors and shapes, the tastes of foods, the feeling of fingers curling around a rattle or a stuffed toy, the

warm wetness of a bath, the swaying motion of the baby carriage — everything is new!

Gradually the baby's need for sleep decreases, and it begins to stay awake longer. A two-year-old child can usually get along with ten or twelve hours of sleep at night and a nap or two during the day. By the age of four or five, most children are ready to give up their daytime naps. The length of time slept at night gets shorter as the child grows older. Teenagers are usually down to about the amount of sleep a grown-up needs.

Most adults feel best if they get about seven or eight hours of sleep a night. But some need more — nine or ten hours. If they don't get that much, they feel tired and grouchy. Other adults feel fine on just five or six hours of sleep a night. (They may take some short naps during the day, in addition.) These "short sleepers" are very busy, energetic people. They don't worry about things very much. When they sleep in the lab, their EEG records show that most of their sleep time is deep, slow-wave sleep. They spend much less time in REM sleep than most people do.

Old people tend to spend less time sleeping at night. They may wake up after four or five hours and feel ready to get up. They sleep less deeply, too. But often they will take naps during the day.

For most people, most of the time, sleep is a natural part of life. At a certain time of the day you feel tired and sleepy. You lie down in bed, and before you know it, you are sound asleep. Then — if nothing wakes you — you will continue sleeping until your body has had enough. Have you ever awakened right *before* your alarm clock rang? Many people can wake up at exactly the time they want to, even without an alarm clock. It seems as though the body has a built-in clock, which tells it when to go to sleep and when to get up.

Night Owls
and Morning Larks

★────────────────────────────★

Some people have trouble sleeping because they are trying to sleep at the wrong time for their bodies. Usually a person's built-in clock is timed to the twenty-four-hour cycle of day and night. Normally you are wide awake and active during the daytime, and you sleep at night. Your whole body works best during your waking hours; your muscles are strongest, your reactions are fastest, and your mind is sharpest during this time. For people whose body clocks are adjusted to this twenty-four-hour day/night cycle, most of the body systems have a low around four o'clock in the morning. The body temperature is lowest then, too. After that, the various parts of the body start getting ready to wake up. But some people's body clocks seem to run differently. When everybody else is ready to get up in the morning, their bodies are still feeling low. They don't start to feel energetic until late afternoon or evening, when other people are starting to get a little tired. When a normal bedtime comes, these late-night people are still going strong. If they try to go to bed at a normal bedtime, they will just lie awake until about two or three in the morning, when their bodies finally feel like going to sleep.

Sleep researchers call these late-night people *night owls*, and they call people who wake up early and feel energetic in the morning *larks*, because larks are birds that wake up early in the morning and sing. The owls of the animal world get along very well sleeping through the day and hunting at night. But, unfortunately for the human owls, our world seems to be made for larks. School and work start early in the morning. In hospitals, patients are often awakened very early in the morning — even earlier than they would normally get up. That is convenient for the hospital workers, but it can be bad for the patients. If you are sick enough to be in a hospital, you need plenty of sleep to help your body get well.

When the night owls grow up, some of them are lucky enough to find a life-style that fits their body clocks. They can take college courses at night, and they may be able to find a job with a late shift. But the rest of them have sleep problems as they try to live in time with the larks. Some doctors think that owls can reset their body clocks. They say the trick is to go to bed *later* each day. For a while the problem seems to get worse, since the person is sleeping when most people are awake, and awake when most people are asleep. But eventually their bedtime shifts to a

normal one. If the person goes to bed the same time every day after that, the body clock learns to keep to its new time.

Shift workers have special sleep problems. They may work days one week and nights the next. As soon as their body clock gets used to one time schedule, the schedule changes again. Some people can adapt to shift work, but others can't. They have such bad sleep problems that they might be better off getting a new job.

When You Can't Sleep

Many things can upset a normal sleep routine. If something very bad happens, worries and fears can keep your mind too busy to let you fall asleep. Happy excitement can have the same effect. You may find it hard to go to sleep the night before you are due to leave on a vacation trip. Loud noises, like jet planes flying overhead or construction workers drilling in the street outside, may also keep you from sleeping. Even a soft noise, like the hum of a fan or the ticking of a clock, can keep you awake. During the day you wouldn't even notice it, but at night, when you are lying in bed in the dark, and everything is quiet, these soft sounds may seem very loud. Sleeping in a different bed or an unfamiliar room can also keep you awake. Many people have trouble sleeping the first night on a vacation trip. The pain of an injury or the discomfort of an illness can also keep you from sleeping.

There is a part of the brain called the *reticular activating system*, or *RAS*, which acts as a sort of message center. Deep inside the brain, the RAS receives messages from all parts of the body: messages about sounds that the ears hear, sights that the eyes see, tastes and smells, the feeling of things that touch the skin, and sometimes feelings from inside the body, like the pain of a stomachache. Normally many different sense messages are coming in at once. If you had to think about all of them, your brain would get confused. So the RAS sorts through the messages that come in and picks out the most interesting, unusual, or important ones. Those are the only messages that are sent up to the thinking part of the brain. When you are getting ready to go to sleep, the RAS starts shutting down. You may be in a noisy room, but you don't hear the noise anymore because the RAS isn't sending those messages to your thinking brain. You can go to sleep with a light on because the RAS stops sending the messages that come in through your eyes. Chemicals called *neurotransmitters*, produced in various parts of the brain, tell the RAS when it is time to shut down for the night. Other neurotransmitters help to wake you up when you have finished sleeping. Worries or excitement can keep you awake by sending a flood of messages from the thinking brain down to the RAS. That keeps the RAS from shutting down.

Most sleep problems last for only a day or two. But sometimes problems go on for weeks or months or even years. People may have trouble falling asleep when they first go to bed. They lie awake for an hour or more. Some people fall asleep quickly enough, but then they wake up in the middle of the night and can't get back to sleep. If you take a long time to get to sleep, or if you wake up before you are supposed to and then can't go back to sleep, you may not necessarily have a sleep *problem*. Maybe you are trying to sleep ten hours a night because that is the "right amount of sleep" for someone your age, but your body really needs only eight hours. The key to whether you have a sleep problem is how you feel when you get up. If you feel rested and ready to start the new day, then you are getting enough sleep. If you wake up feeling

tired and irritable, with aching muscles, and as the day goes on you feel like taking a nap, then you didn't get as much sleep as your body needed.

The term *insomnia* is often used to describe the problem of not getting enough sleep at night. The word actually means *no sleep*, and some insomnia sufferers would say that that is a good name for their problem. "I didn't get a wink of sleep all night," they complain. But when people like that go to sleep in a sleep lab, with electrodes to record their brain waves and show when they are sleeping and when they are awake, it turns out that they were mistaken. The EEG record often shows that the insomnia sufferers are really sleeping a normal amount of time. But they may sleep lightly and wake up several times during the night. When they get up in the morning, they remember the times they were awake and don't remember the times they were asleep. So they think they were awake the entire night. They don't feel rested because they did not get enough deep sleep.

Beating
Sleep Problems

When problems of going to sleep or getting enough sleep go on for a long time, they can make you feel irritable and ill. But what is the best way to solve sleep problems? Is there a pill you can take to give you a restful night's sleep?

Various drugs can help people get to sleep. Your parents or your doctor might give you one to help you through a temporary sleep problem. But sleeping pills should not be taken for more than a few nights. Such drugs cannot really give you normal sleep. Some sleeping pills cut down on the amount of deep sleep, others decrease the amount of REM sleep. But people need both deep sleep and REM sleep in order to stay healthy. If they keep on taking pills, they just feel worse and worse. And yet, they may get hooked on the drugs and think they will not be able to sleep without taking pills.

Sleep experts think it is better not to depend on pills to solve sleeping problems. Instead, people need to develop good sleeping habits. If possible, you should go to sleep in a quiet, comfortable place that is not too cold and not too hot. Sleep clothing should be loose-fitting. You should have a regular routine. Got to bed at about the same time each night, and get up at about the same time each morning. It may be nice to sleep late on weekends, but if you're a person with sleep problems, you may be asking for trouble. Your body clock may get confused, and the extra sleep on the weekends may make you too wide awake to go to bed at your normal time.

Some people find they can get along on a little less sleep at night if they take a short nap or two during the day. But people suffering from insomnia may make their problems worse by napping. If they sleep too much during the day, they may feel wide awake when bedtime comes. And then they feel so tired the next day that they take another nap. Naps are good for you if they help you to feel fresh and rested and don't spoil your normal night's sleep.

Getting enough exercise during the day can help you to sleep well at night. But heavy exercising right before you go to bed is not a good idea. Running or jumping or aerobic dancing gets your body charged up and ready for action, not for sleeping.

People who can't get their sleep problems under control by themselves can go to a special sleep center. There they are asked questions about their sleeping habits and problems, and perhaps they may sleep in

the sleep lab for a few nights, with an EEG machine recording their brain waves. Sometimes there is a physical or emotional problem that doctors can treat. But often all that is needed is to correct some poor sleeping habits.

Sleep centers can help with insomnia and with various other sleep problems, such as sleepwalking, bed-wetting, or nightmares. Finding out the timing of the problem in the sleep cycle may aid in discovering its causes and working out treatments. *Nightmares*, for example, generally occur during REM sleep, while *night terrors* strike in periods of deep sleep. Sometimes drugs that cut down on a particular type of sleep may be used for a while to ease this problem.

You might think that *bed-wetting* occurs during dreams. Actually, though, studies in sleep labs show that it happens during the deeper stages of sleep. Most children learn to stay dry at night by the age of two or three, but some go on wetting much longer — even into their teens. Or a child who has been staying dry may suddenly begin to wet the bed at night again. If the bed-wetting goes on for a long time, doctors look for emotional problems that may be disturbing the child. There may also be physical causes, such as a small bladder or a problem with the nerves that send messages to the muscles that keep the bladder closed. Often, simple exercises can strengthen a child's control over the bladder during sleep. Not drinking liquids before bedtime can help; or drugs may be used for a short time to stop bed-wetting.

Sleepwalking is another problem that starts during deep sleep, not during dreams. Studies of children who sleepwalk usually show that the brain and nerves have not yet developed fully. The controls that normally keep a person limp during sleep are not working properly. Sleepwalkers don't need any special treatment, but they do need to be kept safe. They are not completely aware of things around them, even though their eyes may be wide open. So they must be protected from dangers such as open fireplaces or steep stairways, and doors to the outside should be kept locked. Sleepwalkers may roam around for as much as half an hour and then return to bed. When they awaken, they don't remember having gotten out of bed. Children eventually outgrow sleepwalking as the brain and nerves mature. Sometimes they may sleepwalk again as adults. That usually happens in times of illness or emotional problems.

There are other sleep problems that may also be helped at a sleep center. Some people suffer from a condition called *narcolepsy*: They fall asleep during the day, often very suddenly, because the parts of the brain that normally control sleeping and waking are not working properly. Narcolepsy can be dangerous, especially if a person is driving a car or using machinery at work. But doctors can treat it with drugs and by teaching the person better sleep habits.

Snoring may seem funny, but it can be very unpleasant and disturbing for a person trying to sleep in the same room. Usually snoring is just an inconvenience, but sometimes it can be cause for more serious concern. It may be a symptom of a dangerous breathing problem called *sleep apnea.*

People with sleep apnea stop breathing many times a night, for as long as a couple of minutes. (Apnea means *not breathing.*) This may happen in very young babies, and some have been known to die from it. When doctors suspect that a baby has this problem, they can give the parents a special alarm system. It lets the parents know whenever the baby stops breathing. After a number of months, the baby's breathing system starts to work better, and the apnea attacks no longer occur. Sleep apnea may also be present in older people. Sometimes an operation may be needed to widen the airway in the throat.

Fortunately, most people never have sleep problems serious enough to send them to a sleep lab. But everybody suffers a sleepless night now and then. If that happens to you, the most important thing to remember is: don't worry about it. Worrying about not sleeping can stimulate your RAS and keep your brain so active that you *really* can't go to sleep. Just lie back and try to relax. If you're hungry, you might have a light snack and a glass of warm milk. Milk contains a chemical called *tryptophan*, which is changed into neurotransmitters that tell the brain it is time to go to sleep. Don't eat a heavy meal right before bedtime; that can also keep you awake. And don't drink coffee, cola, or any other drink with *caffeine* in it before going to bed. (Caffeine is a stimulant that keeps the mind active and awake.) You can try counting sheep. Picture their fat, woolly bodies bounding over a fence, one by one. That sounds a little silly, but it often works. The picturing and the counting keep your mind occupied, and counting sheep is boring enough to send you right to sleep!

If nothing works — and after a couple of hours have gone by you still are wide awake — don't fight it. Missing a few hours of sleep, or even a whole night, won't hurt you in the long run. Don't stay in bed worrying about it. Get up and do something. Maybe you can read a book, or watch some TV. (No late-night horror shows, though! Try something soothing to calm down your RAS.) Or get an early start on some of the chores you were planning to do the next day. And then, if you are starting to feel pleasantly tired, don't stay up to read another chapter or finish straightening out your drawers. Trust your body and go to bed. When you're ready, you'll fall asleep.

★ ★ ★

Sleep is a natural part of our lives. It is something that we share with other members of the animal kingdom. It is timed to the daily rhythms of our planet earth, but not bound to the cycles of light and dark. People can fall asleep and wake up in dark caves where no light shines, and they can sleep through the light of the summer-long midnight sun of the far North or South. Astronauts, drifting weightless in their orbits in space, still fall asleep and wake up in regular rhythms, too.

We can't do without sleep — at least, not for very long. Sleep is a time for recharging our batteries, resting and gathering new energy for the day ahead. Cuts and bruises and sore muscles are healed while we sleep. Though our brain has blocked out the sights and sounds of the outside world, it is busy replaying the events of the day, sorting through the new information, and weaving bits of it into the complicated web of memories and beliefs and behavior that makes each person unique. All these mysterious things go on every night, and yet we remember nothing — except perhaps a hint here and there, in the fading mists of dreams.